THE MOON

CARMEN BREDESON

THE MOON

A FIRST BOOK
FRANKLIN WATTS
A Division of Grolier Publishing
NEW YORK / LONDON / HONG KONG / SYDNEY
DANBURY, CONNECTICUT

I would like to thank the following people at NASA who took valuable time away from their jobs to show the magic of the Space Center to me.

—Maxine Sevier introduced me to all of the right people.
—Dr. Carl Allen, Principal Scientist, made my visit to the Lunar Laboratory a truly memorable one.
—Andrea Mosie, geologist, demonstrated so well the techniques and care taken when handling the lunar samples.
—Bruce Hilty led me on a wonderfully informative tour of Mission Control.

Photographs ©: Art Resource: 11 (Firenze Biblioteca Nazionale); Corbis-Bettmann: 33; Don Dixon: 49; NASA: cover, 13, 36, 37, 38, 43, 44 inset, 46, 51; Photo Researchers: 16, 17, (John Bova), 24 (John Foster), 14 (David A. Hardy/SPL), 42 (Mark Marten/NASA), 26 (Andrew J. Martinez), 19 (Kent Wood), 53 bottom (Zuber et al/Johns Hopkins University/NASA/SPL); Stocktrek: 53 top, 55 (Frank Rossotto); Superstock, Inc.: 10, 22, 34; UPI/Corbis-Bettmann: 44 (NASA), 31; Visuals Unlimited: 9 (Arthur Morris).

Library of Congress Cataloging-in-Publication Data
Bredeson, Carmen.
    The moon / by Carmen Bredeson
        p. cm.—(A First Book)
    Includes bibliographical references and index.
    Summary: Describes what people have believed about the moon and what has been learned over time, and presents an overview of the Apollo space program.
    ISBN 0-531-20308-5 (lib. bdg.)   0-531-15911-6 (pbk.)
        1. Moon—Juvenile literature. 2. Project Apollo (U.S.)—Juvenile literature. [1. Moon. 2. Moon—Exploration. 3. Project Apollo (U.S.)] I. Title II. Series
    QB582.B74 1998
    523.3—dc21   96-40226   CIP

CONTENTS

THE MYSTERIOUS MOON

CHAPTER ONE

To our early ancestors, the moon was a mysterious and sometimes frightening light in the sky. Some prehistoric people believed that the sun, stars, and moon were gods who controlled the passage of night and day. Mystified, they watched the moon appear to change shape as it moved from one part of the sky to another.

LEGEND AND SUPERSTITION

The ancient Chinese believed that during the time of a lunar eclipse, a monster was chasing the moon and trying to swallow it. In order to scare the beast, whole villages gathered to shout and bang drums. As the moon gradually reappeared, the people stopped their noise and chanting. They had successfully chased the evil demon away, and the moon was once again safe and whole.

Many superstitions about the moon were passed down through the ages. One legend was that sleeping in the moonlight caused insanity. The term *lunatic* comes from the Latin word *luna*, which means "moon." In Brazil, some village women still shield their babies from moonlight to protect them from lunacy.

Other moon legends have survived to become the topic of horror stories and movies. European folklore tells of a man who turns into a wolf during the full moon and hunts for human beings to kill and eat. The wolf must shed his skin and return to human form before the moon sets, or he will die. In medieval times, many European men were actually tried and convicted of being werewolves.

While some ancient people viewed the moon as magic or worshipped it as a god, others began to observe it and record its movements through space. They kept track of the phases of the moon in relation to the seasons. Some Native Americans called the time during the winter when the wolves were hungry the "Wolf Moon." In the summer, when mosquitoes swarmed, it was the time of the "Moon of Blood."

The moon has long been a source of superstition and myth.

EARLY SCIENTIFIC THEORIES

As humans watched and studied the moon over the centuries, their knowledge gradually increased, and theories about the universe were formed. In A.D. 140, Greek astronomer Claudius Ptolemy said that the Earth was the center of the universe and that everything else revolved around it. That theory was widely believed until Nicolaus Copernicus made some startling statements 1,400 years later. The Polish astronomer said that the sun was at the center of the solar system and that the Earth, moon, and stars revolved around it. His ideas, which were later proven to be true, were not accepted at the time.

In the late 1600s, Italian mathematician Galileo Galilei made drawings of the moon's surface (opposite page) after studying it through his simple telescope (above).

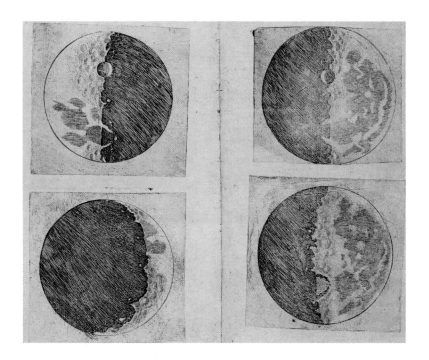

The first real breakthrough in the study of the moon came in 1690. That year, Italian mathematician Galileo Galilei used a simple telescope to study the lunar surface. He saw that the moon was not smooth, but covered with mountains, craters, and valleys. Galileo carefully examined the dark spots on the face of the moon. For years, people thought they were oceans. They named the dark spots *maria*, the Latin word for "seas." Galileo's telescope was not powerful enough to tell what the spots were, so he also assumed they were bodies of water.

THE "CHANGING" MOON

CHAPTER TWO

Gradually, larger and more powerful telescopes were built. Astronomers learned that the maria do not contain water. Instead, these dark areas that cover 16 percent of the moon's surface are filled with lava that had flowed into huge impact craters and then cooled and hardened. Some of the maria stretch for hundreds of miles and are visible from Earth without a telescope.

When we look at a full moon we see what appears to be a face peering down. This is sometimes called the "man in the moon." The dark areas that make up the eyes, nose, and mouth are actually large "seas" of hardened lava.

Today we know that the moon's dark spots,
or maria, are not bodies of water, but
lowlands filled with hardened lava.

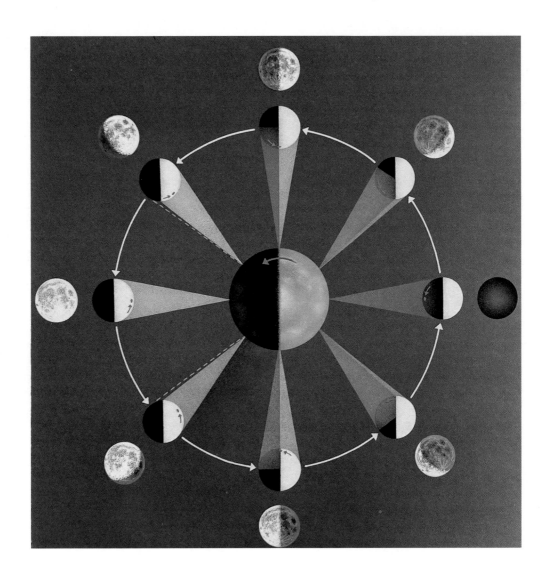

During its 27$\frac{1}{3}$-day orbit around the Earth, the moon appears to change shape because we see different amounts of its sunlit side.

THE MOON'S ORBIT

Astronomers studying the moon were also able to explain some of the mysteries about the moon's shape and its occasional "disappearance" from the sky. The moon appears in different places in our sky because it is constantly traveling in an elliptical (oval-shaped) orbit around the Earth. The trip takes the moon about 27⅓ days to complete. We always see the same side of the moon because it rotates, or turns, only once during each Earth orbit. That slow turn keeps the same side of the lunar surface facing us. By contrast, the Earth makes one complete turn every 24 hours in its 365-day journey around the sun.

WAXING AND WANING

While we always see the same side of the moon, called the near side, we do not always see the same amount of the moon. During its trip around the Earth, the moon's shape appears to change. Actually, the moon itself is not changing. What changes is the amount of sunlight that we are able to see falling on the moon. Since the moon has no light of its own, what we

These photographs show various phases of the moon, including (from left to right) a waxing crescent moon, a waxing half moon, a waxing three-quarter moon, a full moon, a waning half moon, and a waning crescent moon.

see as moonlight is actually sunlight reflecting off the lunar surface.

As the moon travels around the Earth, we see different parts of the sunlit surface. When the moon is between the Earth and the sun, the sunlight falls on the side of the lunar surface that is turned away from Earth. Since we cannot see the far side of the moon, it appears that there is no moon in the sky, and that phase is called a

new moon. We can actually still see a faint out-line of the new moon because a small amount of sunlight bounces off of the Earth's atmosphere and reaches the lunar surface.

As the moon continues its trip around the Earth, its position in the sky changes in relation to the sun. Every day, a little more of the moon's lighted side can be seen on Earth. About a week after a new moon, we can see half of the circle, and a week later, we see the full moon. At this point, the moon is opposite the sun, so light is falling on the entire lunar surface that is turned toward the Earth.

There are about 30 days between one full moon and the next. During the time that more and more of the lunar surface becomes visible, the moon is said to be waxing. Gradually, the moon continues on its path around the Earth. As it shows less and less of its illuminated face to us, it is said to be waning.

"BLUE MOON"

Once every 2.7 years, there are two full moons in one month. This happens because the twelve months in our calendar do not exactly match the moon's cycle. The second full moon in one month is called a "blue moon." This name has nothing to do with the color of the moon, and it is unclear how the term came about. The expression "once in a blue moon" has come to mean something that does not happen very often.

LUNAR ECLIPSES

Occasionally there is an eclipse of the moon, when no sunlight falls on the moon for a short period. To understand what happens during an eclipse, remember that when light shines on objects, shadows are cast behind them. When the sun shines on the Earth, a large shadow, or umbra, is cast into space behind the planet. A

This special photograph shows a lunar-eclipse sequence at 15-minute intervals.

lunar eclipse occurs when a full moon passes through the shadow cast by Earth. Sunlight cannot reach the lunar surface because the Earth and its shadow are in the way.

The darkening of the moon does not happen all at once. Rather, the umbra slowly covers the face of the moon until the entire lunar surface is in shadow. A total lunar eclipse can last up to an hour and a half. While the moon is indeed dark, it still has a deep reddish color that must have seemed ghostly to some of our ancient ancestors.

If only part of the moon's face is shadowed, a partial eclipse is said to have taken place. During a partial eclipse, the moon does not pass entirely into the Earth's shadow, and only part of the surface is darkened. This type of shadow is called a penumbra. It is perfectly safe to watch either a partial or total eclipse of the moon. You should never watch an eclipse of the sun, however, because looking at the sun can permanently damage one's eyes.

THE MOON AND EARTH

CHAPTER THREE

In addition to learning about the moon's phases and eclipses, astronomers also discovered that there was no atmosphere on the lunar surface. On Earth, the air that surrounds us is called the atmosphere. It contains the gases that we breathe, which are primarily oxygen and nitrogen. The atmosphere also acts like a blanket around the Earth. It helps to block the sun's harmful rays during the day and keeps heat from escaping at night. Without the atmosphere, Earth's temperatures would be much more extreme.

Earth's atmosphere also makes the moon appear to be very large at times. When we see a full moon that is just peeking over the curve of

The moon appears huge when it first peeks over
the Earth's horizon because the moon's light
rays are striking Earth at an angle and are
magnified by the Earth's atmosphere.

the Earth, it appears to be huge. That is because
the moon's light rays are striking Earth at an
angle and are magnified by the atmosphere.
When the moon is overhead, the light rays
come straight down and are not distorted by
the curving blanket of air.

GRAVITY AND MASS

Earth's atmosphere is held in place by gravity, a force that attracts objects and matter to each other. On Earth, gravity pulls everything toward the center of the Earth. When you jump on a bed, you do not fly off into space because gravity pulls you back to the mattress. No matter how high you throw a ball into the air, gravity will eventually cause it to fall to the ground.

Earth's gravity is so strong that it also has an effect on the moon, which is an average of 238,857 miles (384,403 km) away. The moon is held in orbit because of the strong pull of Earth's gravity. The amount of gravitational force an object has depends on its mass and on its distance from another object. The greater the mass of an object and the closer it is to another object, the greater its gravitational pull.

Mass is the amount of matter an object has. But you can't always tell the mass of an object by its size. Two objects can be of the same size and yet be of different masses. For example, think of a meatball and a cotton ball that are the same size. Because the meatball has more matter packed into it, it has more mass than the cotton ball. The moon has much less mass than the Earth. It also happens to be only about one-

As this illustration shows, the moon
is about one-fourth the size of Earth.

fourth the Earth's size. If you think of the Earth as
a soccer ball, the moon would be about the size
of an orange by comparison.

Because of its smaller mass, gravity on the
moon is only one-sixth of that on Earth. The gravitational pull on the lunar surface is not strong
enough to capture and hold an atmosphere. As
a result, there is no air or sound on the moon. In
addition, there is no atmosphere to block the

sun's burning rays, so the moon's temperature can reach 260° F (126° C) during a lunar day. At night, with no blanket of atmosphere to keep the heat from escaping, the moon's temperature can fall to –280° F (–173° C).

EARTH'S TIDES

Even though the moon's gravity is rather weak, it is still strong enough to affect the tides on Earth. On the side of the Earth that faces the moon, the water in the ocean is pulled up by the moon's gravity. On the opposite side of the Earth, the water also bulges outward to balance the spinning planet. The two bulges, which produce the high tides twice a day, follow the moon on its journey around the Earth. In between the two high water bulges are low areas, or troughs, that create low tides twice a day.

When you visit a beach, you can see the effects of high and low tides. If you build a sandcastle near the shoreline when the tide is low, the water will gradually rise and cover your creation. On the other hand, if you build your castle along the water's edge at high tide, it will probably still be there the next day. Each day, the beach that you are visiting will have two

The moon's gravity pulls on the Earth
and its large bodies of water, causing
low tides (left) and high tides (right).

high tides and two low tides at about six-hour intervals.

The sun's gravity also has an effect on the Earth's tides, but it is weaker because the sun is about 93 million miles (149 million km) away. The pull of gravity depends not only on the mass of an object, but also on its distance from another object. When the sun and moon are in line with each other, their combined pull produces the highest tides of all. These extremes in water level are called spring tides because the water seems to "spring" from the Earth. During the times when the sun and moon are at right angles to each other they exert a much weaker pull on the water. The result is lower water levels, which are called neap tides.

SLOWING OF THE EARTH

The constant movement of water also has another effect on the Earth. As the water moves back and forth between high and low tides, it rubs against the sand and rocks and produces friction. Just as the brakes on your bicycle produce friction against the tires and slow the bike down, the constant rubbing of the water against the land slows the rotation of the Earth.

With a slowdown rate of less than one second a year, the change is not apparent to any of us. Over time, though, the numbers add up to be significant. Compared to today, the Earth of 900 million years ago turned 30 percent faster and had much shorter days—a day was only 18.2 hours long.

Because the moon is Earth's only satellite and has so much influence on our daily lives, people have always wanted to learn more about it. The development of powerful telescopes gave us close-up pictures of the lunar surface. Scientists studied those pictures and formed theories about what the moon was like. But these were only theories until the arrival of the amazing space age.

VOYAGE TO THE MOON

CHAPTER FOUR

On May 25, 1961, President John F. Kennedy said to the members of the United States Congress: "I believe that this nation should commit itself to achieving the goal, before this decade is out, of landing a man on the moon and returning him safely to Earth."

PREPARATION

After President Kennedy's announcement, the National Aeronautics and Space Administration (NASA) shifted into high gear. Landing a man on the moon in less than 10 years would be an enormous challenge. Seven astronauts were selected to be the first Americans in space. They began months of training as NASA built rockets that would carry human beings into orbit around the Earth.

In order to go into orbit around the Earth, a spacecraft has to be traveling at a speed of 18,000 miles (28,800 km) an hour. If it is going slower than that, it will be pulled back toward the Earth. Try swinging a ball on a string around your head. If you swing it very fast, the string will stay straight as the ball whizzes in a circle. As you slow the motion down, the string sags and the ball eventually falls down because of the force of gravity.

In order to continue on to the moon, the speed of a spacecraft that is orbiting the Earth must be increased from 18,000 to 25,000 miles (28,800 to 40,000 km) per hour. At that speed, the spacecraft is able to escape the pull of Earth's gravity and travel on a path toward the moon. Once it is near the moon, reverse thrusters fire and slow the speed of the capsule so that it can be captured into lunar orbit by the moon's gravity.

NASA's Mercury and Gemini programs were designed to send Americans into orbit around the Earth for gradually longer periods of time. While the astronauts were testing equipment and learning how to maneuver and dock in

NASA had to build extremely powerful rockets in order to send astronauts into space. For a spacecraft to escape the pull of Earth's gravity, it has to reach a speed of 25,000 miles (40,000 km) per hour.

space, unmanned orbiters were sent to the moon to take pictures and land. Scientists wanted to make sure that the moon's surface was hard enough to support a lunar lander.

APOLLO 11

When all of the training was completed and the data collected, the Apollo missions to the moon got underway. The first Apollo flights were test runs to refine all of the procedures. Then the mission that everyone had worked so long and hard for was finally scheduled to blast off. Apollo 11 would be the first attempt ever made to land a person from Earth on the surface of the moon.

On July 16, 1969, astronauts Neil Armstrong, Edwin "Buzz" Aldrin, and Michael Collins blasted into space atop a 363-foot- (111-m-) tall Saturn rocket. Just two and a half hours into the flight, their Apollo 11 spacecraft, *Columbia*, broke free of Earth's gravity and began a 238,857-mile (384,403-km) journey to the moon.

Three days later, *Columbia* went into lunar orbit. Armstrong and Aldrin crawled through a narrow hatchway and entered the lunar module (LEM), the *Eagle.*

Apollo 11's lunar module, *Eagle*, separates from the command module, *Columbia*, to begin its descent to the moon.

FINAL DESCENT

Once inside the *Eagle*, Armstrong and Aldrin separated from *Columbia*, the mother ship. They then fired a rocket that sent them toward the surface of the moon. When the *Eagle* was 300 feet (91 m) away from the landing site, the astronauts saw that they were headed for an area covered with large boulders. It was then that Neil Armstrong disconnected the computers and started to manually control the landing. He flew the LEM over the rock-strewn ground, looking for a safe place to land.

With only 20 seconds of fuel left, he finally settled the *Eagle's* four spindly legs onto the moon. His first message to Earth was "Houston, Tranquility Base here. The *Eagle* has landed!" The site for the first moon landing was Mare Tranquillitatis, or the Sea of Tranquility, one of the dark lunar areas that was once thought to be covered with water.

Neil Armstrong guides the *Eagle* over the moon's rock-strewn terrain, looking for a safe place to land.

A HISTORIC MOMENT

After landing, the astronauts ate a snack and began the job of putting on their bulky spacesuits. With their suits on and their equipment checked, Neil Armstrong opened the hatch. A camera mounted on the outside of the LEM transmitted pictures to 500 million viewers back on Earth. People around the world watched their televisions in amazement as Armstrong made his way down the ladder on July 20, 1969. As his feet touched the ground, he said, "That's one small step for a man . . . one giant leap for mankind."

Fifteen minutes later, Buzz Aldrin came down the ladder and the two men began to set up an American flag and several scientific instruments. Since gravity on the moon is only one-sixth of that on Earth, their 185-pound (83-kg) spacesuits did not slow them down very much. Dressed in their suits, the men weighed 360 pounds (162 kg) on Earth, but only 60 pounds (27 kg) on the moon. The suits were necessary because there was no air on the moon for the men to breathe. Also, the heavy suits shielded the astronauts from burning heat in the sun and frigid temperatures in the shade.

Neil Armstrong took this photograph of fellow astronaut Buzz Aldrin climbing out of the lunar module for the first time.

Astronauts Aldrin and Armstrong planted an American flag in the lunar soil.

COLLECTING SAMPLES

Back on Earth, viewers were glued to their TV screens, hanging on every word that the astronauts spoke. In describing the lunar soil, Neil Armstrong said, "The surface is fine and powdery. It adheres in fine layers, like powdered charcoal, to the soles and sides of my boots."

Nearly all of the moon's surface is covered

The Apollo 11 astronauts discovered that the surface of the moon was covered with fine-grained soil, called regolith.

with fine-grained soil, called regolith. This soil was created when meteors slammed into the lunar surface, pulverizing the rocks they impacted. The astronauts collected samples of the lunar soil and rocks and put them into two special containers that were carefully sealed after they were filled. Scientists at NASA could not wait to get their hands on those boxes.

RETURN TO EARTH

After collecting 50 pounds (22.5 kg) of samples and taking dozens of pictures, the astronauts' two hours outside of the *Eagle* were nearly over. On that first flight to the moon, the crew was allowed only a brief time outside of the capsule because no one really knew how the men's bodies would be affected by their time on the moon.

Before climbing into the lunar module, Neil Armstrong and Buzz Aldrin left an engraved plaque on the moon that read: "Here men from the planet Earth first set foot upon the moon, July 1969, A.D. We came in peace for all mankind."

Once they were settled again in the lunar module, the astronauts prepared to blast off. They had spent a total of 21 hours and 37 minutes on the moon during their historic visit. After firing up the engine, the *Eagle* rose from the lunar surface in a cloud of moon dust. Three and a half hours later, the *Eagle* docked with *Columbia*. On July 22, 1969, *Columbia's* main engines were fired and Apollo 11 began its 60-hour trip back to Earth. On board were two airtight cases full of treasure.

MORE DISCOVERIES

After *Columbia* splashed down in the Pacific Ocean, precautions were taken with the three astronauts and their cargo. While they were still bobbing around in the water aboard *Columbia*, the men scrubbed down with disinfectant and put on special suits. They were then taken by helicopter to a quarantine unit aboard an aircraft carrier, the *USS Hornet*. The only people who were allowed to come into contact with the astronauts for 18 days were a team of doctors. No one knew if the men had been contaminated with strange germs or microbes on the moon.

While the astronauts were sealed away from their friends and families, the airtight containers of moon rocks and soil samples were sent to Houston. Because of their scientific value, they were flown in two different airplanes in case of an accident. When they arrived at NASA, the samples were taken to the Lunar Research Lab. They were placed in nitrogen-filled vacuum chambers, where they were carefully opened and photographed. Each rock and sample of lunar soil was weighed and measured, while closed-circuit TV cameras recorded every step.

In the months that followed, scientists from around the world came to Houston to study the moon rocks. They determined that the rocks and soil samples did not contain any form of life. Now that concerns about possible contamination by strange moon germs were put to rest, the geologists began to analyze the samples. They had plenty of material to study because the supply of lunar material continually grew as the Apollo program continued.

LATER APOLLO MISSIONS

Beginning with Apollo 15, the astronauts no longer had to explore the moon on foot. They were able to use a battery-powered lunar rover to get around. The vehicle went only 7 miles (11 km) per hour, but it allowed the astronauts to drive several miles from their home base.

A lunar rover was used in several
later Apollo missions.

Apollo 15 landed on an area of the moon
located in the Apennine Mountains, which soar
15,000 feet (4,572 m) above the lunar land-
scape. During one of their buggy rides, the
astronauts found a white rock sitting on a
pedestal-like platform. After they brought it
back to Earth, the ancient moon rock was found
to be more than 4 billion years old. Around the
lunar laboratory, it came to be known as the
"Genesis Rock."

Astronauts aboard Apollo 17 found an unusual area of orange soil during their explorations. Later analysis showed that the samples were 3.5-billion-year-old orange glass beads. They were formed from volcanic fountains that sprayed out of the lunar core during a period of violent upheaval on the moon. The Apollo 15 astronauts had also discovered similar glass beads, except that theirs were green due to a different mineral content. In all, the twelve Apollo astronauts who walked on the moon brought back a total of 842 pounds (379 kg) of lunar samples.

"Genesis Rock," a lunar sample brought back by the Apollo 15 astronauts, is an anorthosite, the oldest type of rock found on the moon.

The Apollo 17 astronauts discovered an unusual area of orange soil on the moon (top) that was found to be made up of 3.5-billion-year-old glass beads (left).

LEARNING FROM MOON ROCKS

CHAPTER SIX

Today, the moon samples are housed at NASA's Lunar Laboratory in Houston, Texas. The steel-lined rooms have thick concrete walls, massive doors, and a sophisticated security system. The two main areas that make up the repository are called "clean rooms." The air in those rooms is filtered, and special clothing must be worn inside the chambers. All the precautions are taken to keep contaminants from being carried into the area.

UNTOUCHED BY HUMAN HANDS

Trays filled with rocks, dust, pebbles, and sand that were collected on the moon fill the stainless-

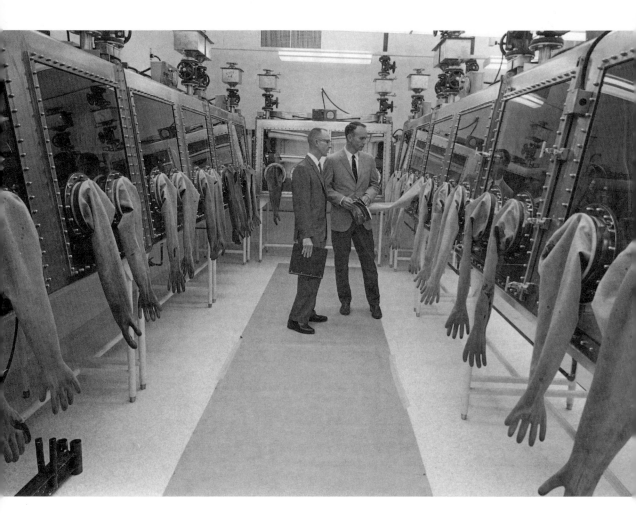

NASA's Lunar Laboratory in Houston, Texas, houses lunar samples in special vacuum chambers filled with nitrogen. The moon samples are touched only with gloves— never directly by human hands.

steel cabinets in the laboratory. Each cabinet is a vacuum chamber filled with pure nitrogen. Since the moon has virtually no atmosphere, the samples cannot be stored in the air found here on Earth or they would deteriorate. Geologists work with the lunar material by placing their hands and arms into long rubber gloves built into the cabinets. Human hands never touch the moon rocks directly.

In the first room of the laboratory, lunar samples are prepared for museums and scientists who request the material to study or display. In the second room of the laboratory, the moon samples that have never left the grounds are stored. After more than 25 years, there is still much to be learned from the material that was brought back to Earth by the Apollo missions. Machines and technology improve with each passing year, making it possible to discover new things about the samples.

CLUES TO THE MOON'S ORIGIN

When the moon rocks were first studied in 1969, it was not possible to accurately tell how old they were. Since that time, dating methods have been invented that tell us the lunar material is between 3.2 billion and 4.6 billion years old. While there have been several theories about how the moon was formed, many lunar scientists now believe that about 4.5 billion years ago, an object the size of Mars came blasting through the blackness of space. In its path was a still-forming planet that would one day be called Earth.

The impactor got closer and closer until it struck its target, not head-on, but with a glancing blow to one side. When the two bodies collided, a fiery explosion sent a stream of blazing material shooting into space. Some of the debris settled into an orbit around the planet. The material gradually combined into a mass of molten rock that melted together to form the moon.

For many millions of years, the moon's surface was covered with a boiling ocean of molten lava, called magma. As the magma cooled, a thick crust formed on the lunar surface. Occasionally, parts of the still-hot inner core broke through the crust and sent huge fountains of volcanic material shooting upward. After the initial explosions were over, lava poured from the holes in the lunar crust and ran in rivers along the surface of the moon.

The moon's craters were formed by meteorites slamming into the lunar surface.

The lava collected in low-lying areas, where it hardened. Many of these bowl-shaped regions were impact craters that had been gouged out of the moon as meteorites slammed into the lunar surface. In time, the violent upheaval on the moon stopped. An occasional volcano still erupted, but that occurred only rarely. By about 2 billion years ago, the moon's appearance was similar to what we see now.

LEGACIES OF THE MOON'S BIRTH

As we look at the moon, we see the dark maria, surrounded by the lighter-colored highlands, which are called terrae. Anorthosites, the moon's oldest rocks, are found in these areas. These ancient rocks were formed during the moon's birth, about 4.6 billion years ago.

Samples from the dark-colored maria, called basalts, are younger than the ancient anorthosites. The basalts formed after volcanoes spewed rivers of lava onto the lunar surface. Yet another kind of moon rock, called breccia, was formed during meteorite impacts. Breccia are a combination of matter from meteors that fused together with part of the lunar surface after impact.

There are examples of each of the three kinds of moon rocks in the Lunar Laboratory in Houston. All of the lunar samples are older than any rocks found on Earth. That is because the moon has not been geologically active for billions of years. What was formed during the moon's active phase has stayed the same for millennia.

Close-up views of a basalt (left)
and a breccia (right)

On Earth, erosion and shifting continents have ground down the original planetary material. Old mountain ranges have worn away, while new ones have taken their place on the Earth's surface. Unlike the moon, our world is constantly changing. By carefully studying the ancient moon rocks, we can learn about the birth of our own planet.

MOON EXPLORATION TODAY

CHAPTER SEVEN

After the Apollo program ended in 1972, no more astronauts traveled to the moon. Interest in Earth's satellite did not lessen, however. In time, scientists decided to take another look at the lunar surface. Because money was tight and piloted missions were expensive, unpiloted space probes were built to fly around the moon and collect information.

CLEMENTINE

In February 1994, a 500-pound (225-kg) probe called *Clementine* entered lunar orbit. For 71 days, the small spacecraft flew around the moon. Its miniature cameras took more than 1.5

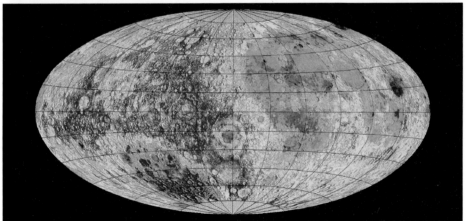

Photographic images taken by the
spacecraft *Clementine* (top) were put
together to form detailed pictures of the
moon's entire surface (bottom).

million images of the lunar surface and beamed them back to Earth. The clear images were put together to make a detailed picture of the entire surface of the moon. The pictures showed for the first time that the bottom of a deep crater at the lunar south pole may never get any sunlight.

Some of the signals sent back by *Clementine* suggest that ice may be present in the huge crater. Ice on the moon would be a very valuable resource. It could be melted and used for growing plants in lunar greenhouses. Also, hydrogen and oxygen could be extracted from the water to make rocket fuel. Having a source of water on the moon might make a colony on the moon possible. With its own supply of rocket fuel, the moon might even become a lunar "gas station" for further space exploration.

LUNAR PROSPECTOR

In order to find out if ice really exists on the moon, NASA planned to launch *Lunar Prospector* in September 1997. The drum-shaped, 513-pound (231-kg) spacecraft would remain in lunar orbit for one to three years. State-of-the-art scientific instruments would measure the moon's chemical makeup along with its magnetic fields

An illustration of *Lunar Prospector*

and gravity fields. During its flight, *Lunar Prospector* will fly over the moon's south pole and carefully examine the deep craters. Data from the spacecraft should make it clear whether or not there is ice present in that frigid territory.

Through the efforts of NASA and the intrepid astronauts, we have learned a great deal about the moon. Moon rocks are studied in laboratories around the world. Many are on display in museums for the public to view. In two places in the United States, the curious can even touch a piece of the moon.

At the NASA Visitor's Center in Houston, Texas, and the Smithsonian's Natural History Museum in Washington, D.C., excited children and smiling adults wait in line around the moon rock exhibits. Many grow quiet when it is their turn to slide a finger or two across the shiny, black rocks inside the display cases. In spite of all of our scientific knowledge, there is still something magical about touching an actual piece of the moon.

FACT SHEET ON THE MOON

Symbol for the moon—))

Age of the moon—4.6 billion years

Average distance from Earth—238,857 miles (384,403 km)

Average speed around Earth—2,300 miles (3,680 km) per hour

Diameter—2,160 miles (3,456 km)

Length of time for the moon to orbit Earth—27 days, 7 hours

Length of time for Earth to orbit the sun—364¼ days

Period of one new moon to the next new moon—29.5 days

Surface gravity—about one-sixth that of Earth

GLOSSARY

Anorthosites—light-colored rocks that form the ancient highlands on the moon

Apollo Program—American lunar-exploration program designed to land astronauts on the moon, 1967-1972

Atmosphere—a gaseous blanket that surrounds some planets and moons

Basalt—dark rock formed from hardened lava; present in the dark basins of the moon

Breccias—lunar rocks formed from crushing and mixing during meteorite impacts; contain pieces of many other rock types

Gravity—the force that attracts objects to each other

Impact crater—bowl-shaped pit on the surface of a moon or planet made by the collision of a comet or meteorite

Lava—molten rock that rises to the surface of a planet or moon after a volcanic eruption

LEM—lunar excursion module that landed astronauts on the moon

Lunar eclipse—occurs when the Earth passes between the moon and the sun, blocking sunlight to the moon

Lunar phases—the amount of moon that we see depending on how the sunlight is striking the lunar surface

Mare—any of the flat, dark areas on the surface of the moon; from the Latin word for "sea"; the plural form is maria

Mare Tranquillitatis (Sea of Tranquility)—site of the first Apollo moon landing

Mass—the total amount of matter contained in an object

Meteorite—a meteor that reaches the surface of the moon or the Earth

Orbit—the curved path of one body around another, such as the moon around the Earth or the Earth around the sun

Regolith—layer of rock fragments and dust that covers most of the surface of the moon

Rotation—the amount of time it takes for a celestial body to make one complete turn on its axis

Terrae—bright lunar highlands

Umbra—the shadow cast by a planet or moon

Weightless—not feeling the effects of gravity

FOR FURTHER READING

BOOKS AND PUBLICATIONS

Baker, David. *Danger on Apollo 13*. Vero Beach, Florida: Rourke Enterprises, Inc., 1988.

Cortright, Edgar, ed. *Apollo Expeditions to the Moon*. Washington, D.C.: National Aeronautics and Space Administration, 1975.

Planetary Materials Curation at NASA JSC. Houston: NASA Johnson Space Center, 1995.

Shepard, Alan and Deke Slayton. *Moon Shot*. Atlanta: Turner Publishing, Inc., 1994.

Stott, Carole. *Night Sky*. London: Dorling Kindersley, 1993.

Watters, Thomas. *Smithsonian Guides: Planets*. New York: Macmillan Company, 1995.

ONLINE SITES

Apollo Missions to the Moon
http://garbo.uwasa.fi/pc/gifapoll.html
An online photo album of clickable images from the Apollo missions to the moon. Dozens of photos of the earth, moon, astronauts, and spacecraft, with dates and descriptions.

The Moon

http://seds.lpl.arizona.edu/nineplanets/nineplanets/luna.html

Lots of links and images, as well as theories about the moon's history and composition. Embedded links in the text provide more information.

The Moon

http://www.isr.co.jp/solarsystem/earth.html

Incredible collection of information and images: introduction and history, statistics, movies, moon and earth photos, catalog of craters, and more.

National Space Science Data Center Photo Gallery: Moon

http://nssdc.gsfc.nasa.gov/photo_gallery/photogallery-moon.html

All kinds of clickable images of the moon, including false-color and infrared photos. Read about the Apollo, Galileo, and Clementine missions.

Phases of the Moon

http://www.mines.edu/students/j/jromano/space/luna.html

Phases of the moon every day of the current month.

SKY Online Eclipse Page

http://www.skypub.com/eclipses/eclipses.html

Learn all about lunar and solar eclipses. Select a date and see images of the eclipse. View animation of eclipses and the planets, plus all eclipses between A.D. 1500 and 2500.

INDEX

Numbers printed in *italics* indicate illustrations

ABOUT THE AUTHOR

Carmen Bredeson has a BS in secondary education /English and Journalism and a MS in Instructional Technology/Library. She is a former high-school English teacher. She has spent many years raising funds and promoting public libraries in Texas. She is married to Larry Bredeson, a research engineer, and is the mother of a son and a daughter. The Bredesons live near Houston, Texas. Bredeson is the author of a dozen nonfiction books for middle-school readers.